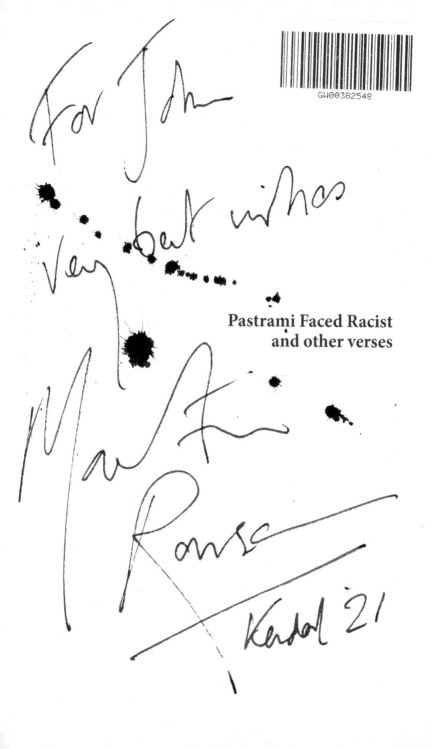

For John

very best wishes

**Pastrami Faced Racist
and other verses**

Martin Rowse

Kendal '21

Pastrami Faced Racist
and other verses

Martin Rowson

Smoke
STACK
BOOKS

Smokestack Books
1 Lake Terrace, Grewelthorpe, Ripon HG4 3BU
e-mail: info@smokestack-books.co.uk
www.smokestack-books.co.uk

Several of the following
originally appeared in the
Independent on Sunday

ISBN 9781999827687

Smokestack Books
is represented
by Inpress Ltd

For my old English teachers
John Fraser and John Steane
and, slightly contritely,
A.N. Wilson.

And, as ever,
for Anna, Fred and Rose,
with all my love.

Contents

Part I: Metrical Rants
Pastrami Faced Racist   11
Hugo from Stowe   17
The Iron Mash of Anarchy   22
A Song for Burns Night   30
Angleterre Profonde   33
Brexit   38
Racism   39
Alliteration   40

Part II: The Abuses of Literacy: Scenes from Literary Life
Barry   45
Charlotte   46
Alain   47
Andy   48
Dan   49
Baz   50
Baron   51
Anabelle   52
Ian   54
KKK   55
The Heart of the Matter   56
How the Good News was Brought from the Frankfurt Book Fair   58
Launch   59
Soho   60
Lest We Forget   63
Cargoes   64
Four Poems about Hay-on-Wye   66
Lines Composed by Dylan Thomas   72
Never Invite A.N. Wilson to Tea   73
Envoi   74

Part III
Short Sharp Shock   79

Part IV: In Brief
Clerihew   89
Love Poem   90

Part I
Metrical Rants

Pastrami Faced Racist

Pastrami faced racist
Basted in baseless
Hatred for faceless
Natives of nameless
Faraway places
Your hatred embraces
Haitians and Thracians,
Laotians, Croatians
With your animadversion
For Persians and Asians
Even Bellarussians
Plus all non-white faces.

Uppercase Statements
Fill all blank spaces
On newspaper pages
Embracing your rage
And deftly showcasing
The in-your-face shamelessness
Of sub-standard statesmen's
Pasty embracing
Like game for the chase
Of hatreds you baste in
Which in your case has
Achingly made
Your furious face
As red as Pastrami.

But Pastrami faced racists
All know their places
Embracing their station
So show no aversion
To faces more gracious
From faraway places
Wreathed in fine laces
Whose soft hands clutch maces
For Kings, Queens and Aces
Need grovelling abasement
Though this self-effacement
Frankly disgraces
The baseless race hatreds
Of racists with faces
Of a hue that's as red as
Pastrami.

So what is the ratio
Between racist passion
And base genuflection?
Is knowing your station
The fuel for reaction,
To make sure your place is
Not quite as basic and
Beastly and graceless
As the gays and the races
And the reds who write plays
And the women whose place is
To not ever gainsay
Your baseless race hatreds?

But tell me, how loud
Would be your hip-hoorays
If some auto-de-fés
Finally saw off the gays
And those Muslimic Beys
And the benefit cheats
Who are worse than the Krays
And the strays and the
General habitués
Of an England betrayed
By not being au fait
With what you think's OK
Which is just to portray
The Pastrami red-faces
Of hatred filled racists
Like you?

Be prepared for your fate.
For if Britain gets Great
Like you want it to – Mate,
There'll be no one to hate
And no one to rate
As debased, a disgrace,
Lower down in their place
Because of their race
Or the look on their faces
Unreddened by basting
In baseless race hatred
To look red as Pastrami.
Like yours.

So, Pastrami-faced racist
If that is the case is
It worth being basted
In dark baseless hatreds?
Just take up macramé
Or try origami
And ignore the barmy
Seductions of smarmy
Fascistic swami
Swim with the tsunami
Of races all chasing a place
Close to Grace.

Though if you can't face
The notion that nations
Can fashion elation
Without your impatience
For fullscale obeisance
To crass racist hatreds
Of the kind that make faces
Go red as Pastrami –
If you want our adherence
To a general clearance
Of all that's divergent
From you, then I urgently
Gently thus phrase it,
As you're basted in hatred
So deep that your face is
As red as Pastrami,
If you're after the lot of us
Then it's you and whose army?

Pastrami-faced racist
Basted in baseless
Hatreds for faceless
Natives of nameless
Faraway places
Back off
Then calm down
And with our assistance
And your own acceptance
To give up resistance
To our co-existence
Your face's tumescence
As red as Pastrami
Will gradually fade to,
Say,
Danish Salami.

Hugo from Stowe

for Kitty

Why is it that wherever I go
I always see someone called Hugo, from Stowe,
Who although his schooldays were long long ago
Shines like a pyre with their bright afterglow?

He's enriching the rich by investing their dough
In a hedgie hegemonic portfolio
In faraway countries about which we know
Fuck all, though in Phuket or down Mexico
With the spoils of his expertise you'll find Hugo
Bellowing in bars in familiar tableaux
'Hey dudes! Where round here can a chap score some blow?'

That's Hugo from Stowe. Yes, Hugo from Stowe,
Bobbing along on the soft undertow
But why is that wherever I go
I'll always see someone called Hugo, from Stowe?

He's working in PR advising Nouveaux
How to ponce with princesses out on the Lido
Or how to chase foxes and gun down a doe
While schooling the oiks how to drawl 'Tally-ho!'
Next he lies for some cunts who are worse than Nero
So their crimes won't exclude them from making a show
At a summit for other cunts in a chateau
Where a President and a Generalissimo
With more blood on their hands than a mafioso
Will stitch up a pitch in which the Status Quo
Pertains, so the World's safe for Hugos from Stowe.

Oh Hugo from Stowe! Hugo from Stowe!
Why is it that wherever I go
Bobbing along on the soft undertow
Is Hugo from Stowe? Here's Hugo from Stowe

Advising the starving which cash crops to grow
So the billions their kleptocrat governments owe
Will easily, ceaselessly, oilily flow
As slithery as eels in the far Sargasso
Into the pockets of Hugo from Stowe
But if that goes tits up and his fortunes fall low
He'll service financially any poor schmo
To invest in a pension plan bonobos know
Won't mature til the mark's in his final death throe.
Thanks Hugo from Stowe! That's Hugo from Stowe!
And I don't have to be Quasimodo
To have had a hunch how far you, Hugo, will go
Braying away in your loud, loose argot
How you've just bought the nanny a new Mondeo
Or selling antiques to old fools in Ludlow,
Titillating *The Tatler* with how the trousseau
Of Lady Atalanta So-and-So
Was spattered with spunk during fellatio
Before their vows were exchanged, doncha know,
Or writing some shit for The Spectator though
Your step-mother this year's a Filipino
While Ma's in Gstaad with a fresh gigolo
But your skin is as soft as the pure, un-skied snow
And your lips wet and scarlet as vintage Bordeaux
And your tousled hair blonder than Bridget Bardot
And your palms are as greasy as chicken gumbo
And the lines of coke rather symmetrically go
With the stripes on your pants tailored in Saville Row
As they have been for each generation of beau
Called Hugo. From Stowe. And is it de trop
That for a millennium, wherever you go
Bobbing along on the soft undertow
There've always been Hugos like Hugo from Stowe.

And nobody else ever seems to shout 'Whoa!'
On your conquering poncing, O Hugo from Stowe
Although one day we all might rise up from below
And in the encompassing imbroglio
As you're strung from a lamp post your spirit will flow
Through the Earth (which you own) and – a bit of a blow –
Your complacency hastens your fall through limbo
Til chastened perhaps you reach INFERNO.

And infernally throned with a sulphurous halo
Lighting up his foul face with a sickening glow
As he languorously chews on a pope's nuncio
Sits SATAN to judge to you, O Hugo from Stowe,
And the cost of each effortless cheap quid pro quo
Which by and large kept you impervious to woe
Keeping bobbing along on the soft undertow
Living life with the ease of a seal on a floe;
From the second dear daddy's jizz, in utero,
First fashioned your genes into an embryo
With the promise of Silver from Eldorado
Beaten into a spoon for your gob as you grow
While the womb in which you gestated, you know,
Was designed, like your school, by Palladio....

O Hugo from Stowe, yes Hugo from Stowe,
With your bristling birthright of braggadocio
Through the blood of your fore-fathers' gurning gung-ho
You sweep cross our land like a hot sirocco
Desiccating to dust each uprooted hedgerow,
Reducing to ashes each Joanne & Joe
Caught in the force of the pyroclastic flow
Of your cavernous charm, your easy ego,
In this fucked, fractured, feudal archipelago
THE TIME FOR YOUR JUDGEMENT HAS COME! Down you go!
Lord Satan will doubtless give you the heave-ho
To the deepest pit wherein you'll burn like tallow
For your manifold faults while alive... Oh, hello!
Hugo thinks as he looks at Old Nick: Don't I know

That face from somewhere? Wicked! Didn't we row
In School's Eight together when we were at Stowe?
And though Hugo thereafter went to Bristol*
Instead of to Peterhouse (Tintoretto
Was his Part II essay – got a 2:2, ho ho)
As it's not quite top-notch, still you'll never outgrow
The grounding they give you in places like Stowe
For networking shaming a Politburo
To ease bobbing along on that soft undertow
For that is the Way of the World, and it's so
Right down to its heart deep in Hell. So Hugo
With an confident drawl shouts out, fortissimo,
'Love the cloven hooves, Lucy! Now high-five me, bro!'
(Though this should be 'high-two me!' which just goes to show
Maths wasn't his strong point for Hugo, at Stowe).

---

*You'll find the 'l's' silent, for those in the know
Like the 't' at the end of a word like 'harlot'.

The Iron Mash of Anarchy

A Mash-up with PB Shelley, first performed at The Chartist *Editorial Board's annual dinner on 26 January 2018, in an upper room at* The Royal Oak *pub, Borough, South London.*

As I lay asleep quite near Brockley
There came a voice from over the sea
And with great power it forth led me
To walk in the visions of Poesy.

I met MURDER on the way –
Looking like ESTHER McVEY –
Wearing a jewelled diadem
And golden shroud (she'd hired them
Along with a strong graveyard whiff
From Mr Iain Duncan Smith).

The poor and the disabled cowered
Behind her as McVEY devoured
A meal made up mostly of them
Then wiped her lips on her shroud's hem.

And farted. The fart truly stank.
She waved towards a new food bank.
'Behold!' she belched. 'The system works!
The shirker now no longer shirks!'

Behind her shuffled, vast & wailing,
The Troll 'FUCK-UP', aka GRAYLING.
Every footstep where he trod
The ground turned into shit from sod.

For into shit turned all he'd clutch –
He'd been born with a Copros touch –
Excepting for the cash, in billions,

He threw aloft. 'This lot's Carillion's!'
He yelped, as down the money rains
On Stagecoach and on Virgin Trains
Til FUCK-UP's puking up his brains.

Which hit the stinking ground and twitch.
He mouthed 'Bless the Deserving Rich'
And, brainless, clueless, lumbered forth
South-easterlywards, never North.

But halt! There's something he'd forgotten
The huge Troll hugged a misbegotten
Weedy man, a dark excrescence
An anti-thing, an absent presence.
And beaming, introduced the runt:
'This is my twin, Jeremy Hunt!'

Next, writhing past like a disease
And squeaking 'Death to Expertise!'
And looking like a startled quail
Is GOVEY, who is called BETRAYAL.

SLOTH shuffles by, seeks where his grave is,
Looking just like DAVID DAVIS
Questing for Eternal Rest
From haggling to be Second Best.

He yawns, then passes both his socks
To MADNESS, known as LIAM FOX
Who sniffs them with excited squeals
Fantasising new Trade Deals.

And all the cranks, careerists, chancers
Peer with dark, suspicious glances
At the colleagues who they hate
Hoping they won't share they fate.

Yet even while the cliff-edge beckons
Not a single one there reckons
He's as vile as who comes now,
Grunting like a farrowing sow:

AMBITION preens and starts to ponce and
Takes the form of BORIS JOHNSON
Before mutating into Lard
And hissing: 'BREXIT – Soft or Hard?'

And many more destructions played
In this ghastly masquerade.
The fires of Hell had made them crisper
Muttering in a pious whisper:

'Protect the Squillionaires from tax;
Keep all Regulations lax;
Shelter a finance director
By fighting back the Public Sector;

'Protect us from yet more Migration
And threats of Miscegenation
And stuff good folk just know is bad
Like PC Lefties going mad.

'And make the claimants eat their young
While everybody else eats dung
Served up by the *Daily Mail*;
And guarantee that every Gaol
Is understaffed & under pressure
Because the taxpayers' treasure
MUST NOT BE WASTED ON THE POOR
OR THE FECKLESS ANY MORE!

'And outsourcing the air we breathe
To OxyVirgin will relieve
The Deficit so generations
Yet unborn will find our nation's
Very fabric was unfurled
So BrexUK CAN LEAD THE WORLD!'

The foul parade was now quite tired
So had a little snooze. A fire'd
Destroyed the block by which they slept
But things like that had never kept

The likes of them from easeful kipping
And in their peaceful dreams they're skipping
Through fields of wheat just for a joke
And quite free of the Brussels yoke.

In realms of Wakefulness, alas,
Other things has come to pass
For standing in a golden cage
Shackled to a necrophage

The one leader they could afford,
The one they all safely ignored:
The Prisoner that set them free:
THE IRON-MASK OF ANARCHY!

And she wore a queenly crown
And in her grasp a sceptre shone;
On her brow this mark I saw
'I AM GOD, & KING, & LAW!'
(While just below that, I was able
To read the motto 'STRONG & STABLE'.)

And there she stood, it seemed forever
Irrespective of the weather:
Rain and hail and sleet poured down
On her ever-rusting crown,
Then superceded in a bit
By an endless shower of shit.

Awaking then, the vile army,
The foaming mad and simply smarmy,
Drunk as with intoxication
Of the wine of desolation

Took up once more their mad parade
Past closed down shop or fracked up glade
With a pace halting and lame
Offering us more of the same:
The triteness, spite, the easy hate
Which had served them well of late.

O'er fields and towns, from sea to sea,
Passed the Pageant swift and free,
Tearing up, and trampling down ;
Till they came to London town.

And each dweller, panic-stricken,
Felt his heart with terror sicken
Hearing the tempestuous cry
Of the Iron-Mask of Anarchy.

For from pomp to meet her came,
Clothed in arms like blood and flame,
The hired murderers, who did sing
'Thou art God, and Law, and King.

'We have waited weak and lone
For thy coming, Wobbly One!
Our purses are empty, our swords are cold,
Give us glory, and blood, and gold.'

Lawyers and priests a motley crowd,
To the earth their pale brows bowed ;
Like a bad prayer not over loud,
Whispering – 'Thou art Law and God.'

Then all cried with one accord,
'Thou art King, and God, and Lord ;
Anarchy, to thee we bow,
Be thy name made holy now!'

And Anarchy, that trembling Queen
Bowed with an uneven grin
And started to speak with a stammer
To say the best school is a grammar.

Then as their slave she asked once more
Her mob to seize the Bank and Tower,
And was proceeding with intent
To shackle pensioned Parliament

When one fled past, a maniac maid,
And her name was Hope, she said :
But she looked more like Despair,
And she cried out in the air :

'For Christ's sake, just get on with it
And let's get to that lovely bit,
So we can dance and all make merry
Like Jeremy did at Glastonbury!

'My name is Hope, and that's the point
Cos we don't need to smoke a joint
To make this one a special day.
We know there is another way.

'You think neo-liberalism
Is doing fine? Viewed through the prism
Of itself that may be said:
It needs reminding that it's dead.

It needs repeating that the onus
Of England's glory's not the bonus
Of bankers who have banked on failure,
Nor policies just aimed to gaol yer.

Don't despair. Get slightly pissed;
Carry on reading *Chartist*;
Support each other; Organise;
And don't believe the Media's lies.

We all know the Tories are shit
And most of them now suspect it
We also know that Labour's for us
So let's now join in Shelley's chorus...

Altogether now...

RISE LIKE LIONS AFTER SLUMBER
IN UNVANGUISHABLE NUMBER –
SHAKE YOUR CHAINS TO EARTH LIKE DEW
WHICH IN SLEEP HAD FALLEN UPON YOU –
YE ARE MANY – THEY ARE FEW!

A Song for Burns Night

First performed at the London Sketch Club's Burnsnight Supper, January 2016. James Maxton, leader of the Independent Labour Party (ILP) and advocate of Scottish Home Rule, was the subject of Gordon Brown's doctoral thesis.

When Jimmy Maxton, bold and red
And long these years amidst the dead,
Led the ILP they said
THE GUTTERS WILL RUN WITH TEA!
Oh the gutters will run with tea, my boys,
The gutters will run with tea!

From crag to glen to stagnant loch
To grouse moor, thence by cheviot flock
Past Kirk to crumbling tenement block
THE GUTTERS WILL RUN WITH TEA!
Oh the gutters will run with tea, my dears,
The gutters will run with tea!

Stags bleed out in the purple heather
Shot by a banker – we're in this together,
All soaked to the skin – whatever the weather
AND THE GUTTERS WILL RUN WITH TEA!
The gutters will run with tea, old chaps,
The gutters will run with tea!

A-brim with Tunnocks without end
And copies of *The People's Friend*
And tendencies to condescend
THE GUTTERS WILL RUN WITH TEA!
The gutters will run with tea, ma hen,
The gutters will run with tea!

Lairds eye up still more land to seize;
Souls get squeezed by the Wee Wee Frees;
The kids have Congestive Heart Disease
YET THE GUTTERS WILL RUN WITH TEA!
The gutters will run with tea, ye ken,
The gutters will run with tea!

And while you sing 'Scotland the Brave!'
Pissing on Greyfriars Bobby's grave
A haggis explodes in a microwave
WHILE THE GUTTERS STILL RUN WITH TEA!
The gutters still run with tea, with tea,
The gutters still run with tea!

Yet Scotland's reborn! No more interference
From Labour in London, despite the appearance
We've outsourced next year's Highland Clearance
STILL THE GUTTERS WILL RUN WITH TEA!
The gutters will run with tea, bravehearts,
The gutters will run with tea!

For if golf courses cover the crofters' croft
And Maxton's portrait rots in the loft
And your new masters now have our snouts in the trough
THE GUTTERS WILL STILL RUN WITH TEA!
The gutters will run with tea, my love,
The gutters will run with tea!

For from that thin, blood-soaked topsoil
That brought forth Burns and Conan Doyle
(And The Krankies and Frankie and Susan Boyle
And cybernats' craniums crowned in tinfoil;
Though the land's for the lairds and their kin to despoil
And every mile is fucking Royal)
There still might be splashes of North Sea Oil
IN THE GUTTERS THAT RUN WITH TEA!
The gutters will run with tea, MSPs,
The gutters will run with tea!

So Scotland for Aye! For Scottish Progress!
For Braveheart! For Burnsnight, when we overdress!
For Hogmanay too, and wild wild excess
When each puke peppered paving stone will effloresce!
And down with the English and the way they oppress
And to hell with the traitors who didn't vote 'Yes'
And cheers for each penny of EU largesse!
Although between ourselves I wouldn't confess
That these days the monsters aren't all in Loch Ness
Patrolled by goons hired by G4S
AND THE GUTTERS WILL RUN WITH TEA!
The gutters will run with tea, my lads,
The gutters will run with tea!
The gutters will run, the gutters will run,
The gutters will run with tea
And if you don't like it that Red Clydeside's dead,
Have some more tea and a slice of shortbread
For we'll keep on voting til Scotland is free
And Brigadoon's gutters will o'erflow with tea!
And the gutters will run with tea, with tea,
The gutters will run with tea!

Angleterre Profonde

I dived into Deep England
Into the Village Green,
Diving down full fathom five,
Diving in between
The fag butts and the condoms,
Smashed beer mugs from the pub,
Tinnies, tyres and bailer twine,
A deathwatch beetle grub,
Some teeth kicked out on Friday night,
Worm-eaten lengths of wicket,
An old school tie worn as a lie
By some chap at the cricket.

I dived into Deep England
By the churchyard, through the dead,
Through ground ground down by coffins
Of the leaders and misled,
The bones of squires' younger sons'
Aborted sons and daughters
Like buried murder weapons. Further down
The earth's three-quarters
Crammed with milkmaids, ploughboys
And peasants generations deep,
Lied to, lying dying,
That they were just going to sleep,
An ossuarial estuary
That sweated ire and toil
Committed to be eaten
To be shat into the soil
Shat out in that rich dust concealed
By microbes lavatorial
Their thin blood soaking Pastoral mud
Beneath the War Memorial.

I dived into Deep England,
Rural as a dying hare,
Where centuries of history
Lurks in a broken chair.
I dived down to Deep England,
Rustic as a lichened tomb
But not for them's were driven out
And then chained to a loom.
I dived down to Deep England
Owned by classes who won't budge
But accordingly Arcadian
When flogging bags of fudge.

I dived down to Deep England
Where the countryside's so pretty
And a country cot costs such a lot
To a shit big in The City.
I dived down to Deep England
Where the birds sing in the trees
And the fauna are all vermin
And a Pop Star makes some cheese.
I dived down to Deep England
As bucolic as the plague
Where titled deeds and ownership
Are often left quite vague.

I dived down to Deep England
Long since subject to Enclosure
With a maypole left for shelter
To guard you from exposure.
I dived down to Deep England
Where the rules are rudimentary
And the land is simply landfill
To oblige the Landed Gentry,
Where if your labour's casual
And times are getting hard
Be pathetically grateful
You can watch Changing the Guard.

I dived down to Deep England
Cos if strawberries get picked
By Poles in pollytunnels
There's still tenants to evict.
Yet if you're not from round these parts
Nor wedded to the earth
What exactly is your value?
What precisely is your worth?
For this is Deep Deep England
As authentic as a stoat,
As English as a Norman Castle,
With a dark green moat,
As genuine as German bankers
Blasting at the grouse,
As real as asset strippers
In a Tudor peasant's house.

This is Deep Deep England,
Where real England's reeled in
By real and proper Englishmen
And women, kith and kin,
Who voted leave as they believe
Down to their English roots
We need to take Deep England back,
Amidst these rotting fruits,
Deep Deep Deep Deep England!
If it's lost we'll be bereft
At losing this sweet monument
To a thousand years of theft.

I dived down to Deep England
Where the poor man's at his gate
And the rich man counts his profits
From the new trading estate.
The land's there to make money,
Its harvests made for scoffing,
Its creatures made for blood sports
And its caps all made for doffing.

I dived down to Deep England
Where the smocks are made of nylon
To dress the modern peasants when
They're polishing a pylon.
I dived down to Deep England
Where they think their Queen's Titania,
The Land of Cockeyne's our Cocaine
And we all live in Narnia.

I dived down to Deep England
So far down I got to Hell
And glanced over my shoulder:
And saw nothing left to sell.
I was drowning in Deep England
Which is deeper than it seems,
Though shallower than the head on
Warm flat beer of which she dreams.
I was drowning in Deep England;
Hit the surface; gasped for air
And choking looked around and saw
Somewhere that wasn't there.

I sank into Deep England
For the third and final time
And a church clock stuck at ten to three
Did not proceed to chime.

Brexit

Leave means Leave
And Yes means Yes
And East means East
And West means West
And Leave means Leave
And No means Yes
And Leave means Leave
And More means Less
And Leave means Leave
And Day means Night
And Leave means Leave
And Black means White
And Leave means Leave
And Left means Right
And Leave means Leave
And White means White
And Leave means Leave
And Might means Right
And Leave Means Leave
And Night means Night
And Leave means Leave
And Less means More
And White means White
And This means War
So leave it out
What Brexit means
Is Leave means Leave
And Heinz means Beans.

Racism

Any Paki, coon or yid'll
Laugh out loud until they piddle
When they hear how brave Rod Liddle
TELLS IT LIKE IT IS. Their widdle
Streams in jets into the middle
Of the dance floor where Rod Liddle
Splashes round to Murdoch's fiddle,
Splish-sploshing as he asks this riddle:
'WHAT'S BLACK AND SPREADS HATE?' Any squid'll
Reply 'the ink with which Rod Liddle
TELLS IT LIKE IT IS!' Hey diddle
Tweedle twaddle fiddly-twiddle
Drones on Rupert Murdoch's fiddle,
Faddle foddle loddle Liddle!
Who'll laugh? Any coon or yid'll,
Til they drench themselves in piddle
When they read how brave Rod Liddle
TELLS IT LIKE IT IS. Go diddle...

In the interests of full disclosure, it should be recorded that in 2002 the author sent Rod Liddle a copy of a cartoon featuring Mr Liddle, for which service he was promised a bottle of wine in lieu of monetary recompense. At the time of going to press, no such bottle of wine has yet been received.

Alliteration

Boris Johnson, Arsehole Adolf, Bannon's braying Brexit bitch, burqua butcher, Cloying Classical cum-stain of Cataline Calamity, Dionysus of Deceit, Elephantine Etonian erk, Fellow-travelling funster fascist of the fuck-up Falange, Git, gurning gimp, Ganymede of ghastly, Haircut Hitler, Incubus of the Infernally, incontinently imbecilic, Joyless joke-free jerk-off Judas, Ku Klux Kaiser of Kitsch, Leonidas of Lies, Leave louse, Minge-maned masturbating manboy of mediocrity, Needily Narcissistic Nero of Nowhere, Otiosely oratorical orang-utan, Preening pratfalling Putinist ponce, Quisling quit git, Rubbish Robespierre, Resignation rat, Romulus of racism, Sniggering smirking Scylla of Shit, Truth-free Tory tosser twat, Ustasha uhlan of ugly, Verruca on the Verifiable, vile virtue virus, Wotan of the wantonly woeful, Xerxes of Xenophobia, Yellow yak of yuck and Zero Zeus has asserted that after leaving the European Union Britain will once more take its place in the community of nations as some kind of latter-day buccaneer.

Personally I wouldn't let the fucker near.

Part II

The Abuses of Literacy:
Scenes from Literary Life

Barry

BARRY, once of Beecham Klein,
Knew all about the Bottom Line,
Downsizing and Penetration,
Spread sheets, Flip Charts, Share, Location;
And – about books – sod all. So he
Got appointed as M.D.
In charge of Publishing and Stores
For a Concern off Many Shores.

The editors went first before
The authors, then the last book store.
'Behold!' cried Baz, *'THE BOTTOM LINE!'*
The Chairman sniffed, shed tears of brine:
'Who'll do my memoirs now?' he gulped.
And then they had poor Barry pulped.

Charlotte

CHARLOTTE travelled near and far
As a Publisher's PR
Shepherding a novelist
Who, on book tours, got so pissed
He missed Radio Stoke-on-Trent's
'Book Fun' puking in the gents.
(A genius, he missed the sink
Then bellowed 'I need more strong drink!')

Charlotte soon got used to coping
With her author's drunken groping
Until the day his wandering hand
Wandered too far. Her Alice Band
Served in the office of garotte...

But bad-boy authors, she forgot,
Are worshipped, though I don't know why.
She got lynched by the W.I.

Alain

Philosophy's great consolations
Seldom guide the lives of nations
And this in turn leads to despair.
Little ALAIN didn't care
Because he knew each part of life –
To eat a peach or take a wife –
Is much more simple than it looks
If you read the Wise Old Books.

And if this sounds like shit to you
Alain might have thought so too
If sweet thoughts of Boethius
Had helped him spot that speeding bus.

Andy

Agent ANDY played bad cop
At 25% a pop
Handling the kind of chap
Whose teeth require a finer cap,
Whose alimony payments yearned
For huge advances (all unearned).

How they quaked when Andy flew in
Bringing publishers to ruin,
Extorting swag with evil grins
For books bound of remainder bins.

He celebrated one such deal
By going for a lavish meal
And pegged out, though the food was fresh
By choking on his pound of flesh.

Dan

Druggy DAN, the Modern Burroughs,
Ploughed angsty and dystopean furrows
Describing low, revolting fun
While living in NW1.

Too much cholesterol, not smack,
Brought on the fatal heart attack,
Summoned to Eternity,
Not all he was cracked up to be.

Baz

Purist BAZ was young and cold
So eschewed Helvetica Bold
When designing books. 'We're racy!
'So why's this book list so *type-facey*?'
Baz declared. 'And it's absurd
That Space gets compromised by Word!'

The publishers all got his gist.
Okayed his plans for that Spring's list.
But books designed on worsted suede
With beige print on an ochre shade
Cannot be *read*. But can't you see
His own design flaw? *Nor could he.*

They pulped the lot, all Baz's babies,
And then his guide dog gave him rabies.

Baron

They called him BARON, just for fun,
Cos 'is way wiv a rivet gun
And 'ow 'e' made 'is old mum tea
Displayed a kind of Chivlary
In those golden, long-lost days
When 'e slapped ponces for the Krays
And 'elped a chappie 'oo'd been naughtie
Prop up part of the M40.

And though, of course, e'd done 'is time,
'E reaped the true rewards of crime
When 'e told all (but didn't squeal)
For 90K (a three book deal!)
Concluding, 'midst ecstatic clapping,
Baron's life of violent slapping.

(Then he had a heart attack
When GUY RITCHIE slapped his back.)

Anabelle

ANABELLE hailed from the shires
And filed her nails for hours and hours.
But as this wasn't quite the thing
She got a job in publishing
And thus this comely Maid of Sloane
Answered her boss's telephone.
'Yar? Who? From where? You've done a book?
'And we paid you? Super! Look,
He's ackshalay quite busy now...'
Spurned too often by this cow
Several authors hired a chap
Who arranged a slight mishap...
There is a pit deep down in Hell
That's guarded now by Anabelle.

Ian

IAN's fictional detective
(Often seen as a corrective
To the oeuvre of A Christie)
Was bitter, glum and often pissed. He
Prowled the streets, once in a while
Beating up a paedophile
And spilling whisky on his trousers.
Crime's not like that in country houses.
There it tends to be less gritty
In light of which it was a pity
That one weekend a candlestick
Did for Ian in a tick.
Whoever dunnit (none did see)
Dunnit in the conservatory.

KKK

Even the best book burning plan
By members of the Ku Klux Klan
Who seek conditions ante-bellum
Through the combustion of velum
Can end in tears. It might be felt
In regions of the Bible Belt
That you just do not get folks turning
Up to join in your book burning
When nobody round here – hell, look! –
Has ever actually owned a book.*

*Don't think about the torments liable
To ail you if you burn *The Bible*.

The Heart of the Matter

We know all published books are dross,
And while this makes me very cross –
Enough, indeed, to cry '*J'accuse!*'
Against the teeming multitude
Of publishers and novelists
And agents, each of whom persists
In burdening our burdened breed
With more than we can ever read,
Along with booksellers and reps
And critics who never take steps
To free us from this ghastly stuff,
Hold up their hands and cry 'Enough!' –
To curse just this bunch makes no sense.
Contributory negligence
Points out another bunch of bleeders:
WHAT ABOUT THE FUCKING READERS?

WHASSAT? JUS' GIVE ME HALF AN HOUR TO FINISH THIS PAGE OF "ATLAS SHRUGGED"...

How the Good News was Brought from the Frankfurt Book Fair Back to an Office in Soho Square

I fell in the taxi, and Toby, and he;
I shuddered, Nick shuddered, we shuddered all three;
'Ze airport?' the driver cried, grinding the clutch;
'With God speed!' we cried, though not one there spoke Dutch;
Behind in the hotel they carried on drinking
And into the night we sped blearily blinking.

Not a word to each other; we hardly could speak;
And none had a sober breath drawn through the week;
I turned to my briefcase and made its girths tight;
When we got through Security I felt like shite;
As tears of pure alcohol streamed down our faces
On the plane we unsteadily lurched to our places.

At Stansted up leaped of a sudden the sun
And against him we stood steaming damply each one;
To a taxi we dashed, though the fare was immense,
Like our hangovers, but we cried 'Fuck the expense!'
And within two short hours the three of us stumbled
Through our offices' doors as our lower guts rumbled.

And all I remember is – so I believe –
How our MD ignored my each latest dry heave,
But looked at the contracts and started to smile
At seventeen books flogged, then after a while
Bellowed 'This Calls for Drinks!', and though my brain hurt
That's how we brought the good news from Frankfurt!

Launch

Another Party, another Launch,
Another author's expanding paunch;
Forget sales figures, just watch the liggers
All Making Whoopee!

Although he wrote it, his book is crap,
And he's now hit that
Reviewer chap!
He may regret it, but let's forget it
And just make whoopee!

All that sales conference red wine
Which down his throat he's poured!
But hell! This is *his* launch party,
Creation's sole reward!

Who are these people? Where are his friends?
He's now so arseholed he's got the bends!
He's feeling flushed, he's
Been sick on Rushdie!
That's making whoopee!

Soho

If you're down in SOHO and you hark to midnight strike
Snort a line or sip your latte – do just what you like;
Read your phone, BUT DON'T TURN ROUND!
Why not? I'll tell you why
Watch the wall, my darling, as Bohemians lurch by.

Five and twenty brandies, twelve more Gin and Its,
Since the 1950s, in The French or Fitz,
Bohemians have bellowed 'Here's compost in your eye!'
So watch the wall my darling while the pissheads stumble by.

Editing a poetry mag they'll touch you for a quid
You'll never see again because they're drunker than a squid;
They'll shed tears of acidic spite about their wasted lives,
All their unfinished novels and their nine abandoned wives.

No strangers to dingy vice, they all know what a dose is
But shrug it off as every year's a Good Year for Cirrhosis;
Tell you you're their best mate, cadge a fiver, swear to meet,
Then drop you like an empty bottle right in Meard Street.

Drunks like William Donaldson or Jeffrey Bernard,
Loud and unreliable, but somewhat of a card,
Artists, aging authors, part-time poets and flaneurs
Just aware though barely human humanity errs.

That lesson learned, they are long dead of hepatic disease
Yet live once more through necromantic hagiographies,
Preserved in pools of alcohol, soaked through their Abercrombies,
Specked with puke and *punt e mes*, this squad of Soho Zombies.

For though about their crumbling bones the cold clay should have cloyed
We keep these lushes living through our love of *schadenfreude*
Though details of their sordid ill-spent lives frankly appal
A thrill of nausea flushes each who hears their limp footfall.

Six and thirty G & Ts wash through those rotting corses
As spirits neck more spirits down in the Coach and Horses
Toasting the next book about them, 'Vomit in your eye!'
Just watch the wall, my darling, while Bohemians waft by.

Lest We Forget

In this season of Remembrance a troubling thought occurs;
A thought, moreover, which from mawkish orthodoxy errs.
What if the First World War was won in late 1914 –
In short, was done by Christmas – do you think we would have seen
The outpouring of poetry which still can prick a tear
Of sorrow, anger and despair from death and mud and fear?

What if, instead of Owen and Sassoon our boys had spun
Patriotic verses all about killing the Hun,
Hymning that great victory we won through blood and sweat
In sonnets singing of the beauty of the bayonet
So that, instead of weeping, you'd gulp out a callous laugh
And cackle cruel triumphalism by the Cenotaph?

More than half in love with painful deaths of all our foes
We'd hear of Berlin burning and the Kaiser's final throes
And bark out brutal ballads on the Triumph of the West,
As earnestly we'd chorus 'Dulce et Decorum Est',
For of War and War's Pity, all that need be said,
It's a pity all the fucking Germans are not now all dead.

I fear that wouldn't do at all, so here's a stark conclusion:
That Poetry's a parasite that feasts on some vague fusion
Of sentimental wallowing in songs best left unsung
About the homely comforts of eating your own young.
Just think! If all those boys had lived to ripening senility
We couldn't weep at all that verse with such shameless facility.

Cargoes

Part I

Bibliophile of Ludlow near the Welsh Marches
Whose accounts are in chaos and all lie unboxed
Never makes a penny
From his Second Hand Bookshop
Crammed full of First Editions (all slightly foxed).

Stately WH Smith's, trading since Victoria's reign,
Banned books by the dozen at a lawyer's behest.
Profits now falling
On sellotape and paperclips,
Magazines and novels. Well, who would've guessed.

Dirty bloody Amazon, undercutting everyone,
Delivered to your front door before you can blink,
Books, trash & dvds,
Toiletries and barbecues
Discounting '50 Shades of Grey'. Doesn't life stink?

Part II

Easyjet from Stansted heading off to Tuscany
With a seven hour drive to the villa! What a drag!
With a cargo of biographies,
Literary fiction
And stuff you're told to read by a bossy Sunday rag!

Ryanair from Gatwick and days in the departure lounge,
Jetting to the Med and a fortnight in the sun!
With a cargo of '50 Shades',
'50 Shades' and '50 Shades'
And 'Harry Potter' by the bucketload. What fun!

Dirty clapped out Volvo with a dog dying in the boot,
Stuck in endless traffic all the way to Truro
With a cargo of MORE BOOKS
Endless Summer Reading!
Why can't people travel without Books? I know!

Sturdy British Bobbies on the look out for ne'erdowells
Policing all our borders just to stop the rot,
Confiscating rucksacks
Blowing up their contents
After taking out the bloody books and burning the lot.

Four Poems about Hay-on-Wye

I

The Po through Tuscan plains doth gently wend
To lap 'gainst fronded banks in jewell'd Florence
Where Dante, out of love for Beatrice, penned
'Inferno', while the rain fell down in torrents
On Hay-on-Wye, as it does to this day.
Another Florence now reigns in that place
And yearly lures great writers unto Hay
Unlikely though this sounds. Could Dante face
(Were he alive) the journey from his Florence,
Its azure skies, its sun, its scented airs,
To this one? Or would his well-known abhorrence
For lecturing ladies sat in stacking chairs,
Or chatting for an hour with D J Taylor,
Or reading from his books (though for a fee)
Or signing them, or even (ah! Words fail!) a
Portaloo awash with writers' wee
Make him say no to Florence (not Firenze)?
I think so, for it is a certain bet
That though this drives P Florence to a frenzy:
He'd never write 'Inferno'. It's too wet.

67

II

Shall I compare thee to a summer's day?
Don't bother! Can't you see it's pissing down?
And as for all those darling buds of May,
They're now all soaking wet and going brown.
So is this the Pathetic Fallacy
(Where wild emotions fuel the elements)?
Through hate and fear, like Lear, have callous we
Brought down the rain? For Christ's sake, have some sense!
For while we huddle from the Tempest's teeth,
Don't ask why we endure this sodden season,
But conjure up another blasted heath
In Wales, on Wye, and there you'll find a reason.
Man's words, intense (in tents), enrage the sky;
Not deeds, but books, bring forecasts far from fine;
And therefore's wherefore floods engulf the Wye:
When you make Hay the sun will never shine.

III

Roy, despite his many flaws
Was a sucker for applause.
His books weren't great, but he was fresh
And up for it to press the flesh
At Literary Festivals
To show that readers were his pals,
With talks, on panels and on tours,
Proving writers are just whores
Yearning to hear 'How Great Am I?'
And then he drowned in Hay-on-Wye.

IV

for David Miller

O gracious heavens, tell me why
I'm on a train to Hay-on-Wye!
I think that I should rather die
Or get bit by a tsetse fly
Or fuck a fat sow in a sty
Or drive a chisel through mine eye
Or dine at length with Stephen Fry
Or eat a cheese and rissole pie
Or dance with anthropophagi
Or hear the Kraken's sullen cry
Or else a werewolf's hungry sigh
Or wear an Old Etonian tie
Or, in some quicksand, wave goodbye...
Instead I'm off to Hay-on-Wye.

Envoi

Dear God! Now with all passion spent
I'm stuck for hours in Newport, Gwent!

Lines Composed by Dylan Thomas on the 50th Anniversary of his Death

Do not go gentle into that good night!
And so I'll have another for the road!
Rage... I don't suppose you've got a light?
Thanks pal... *men at their end know dark is right*
Because – Oh Christ, I'm gonna chuck my load!
No! Gulp! I'm fine, yes... *into that good night.*
Good men – you're all my pals! – *crying how bright* –
Dear God it is and all! Please dim them now!
Rage, rage against the dying of the light!
What's that? Are you, sir, asking for a fight?
Then step outside! I'll thump you like a cow!
You'll not go gentle into that good night!
What? Sorry, no, I'm calm now, I'm alright...
Dedum dedum dedum dedum dedum.
And now that one last drink and then goodnight!
What? I had it fifty years ago? Oh shite!
And I've been dreadful dead since then? Oh bum!
And this is not a hangover? Oh right.
Then I'll go gently into that good night.

Never Invite A.N. Wilson to Tea

Never invite A.N. Wilson to tea!
He'll be oh so polite but just you wait and see!
You'll pass him the last slice of Battenburg cake
Which will prove in his mind you're a frightful old fake!
He'll accept a sweet sherry with hardly a blush
And years later write you're a chronic old lush!
You'll mention your books and he'll gush 'They're divine!'
And think you're a Pooterish, vainglorious swine
(But nip to kitchen and quite without fail he's
Raided the drinks trolley, finished the Bailey's).
At long last he'll leave. You'll peck his pale cheek
And he'll write you have sex sixty times every week.
So never invite A.N. into your gaff:
Your morals are lax and your furniture's naff!
Never ask Wilson down into your pit:
He just can't resist rolling you in the shit!

Envoi

The time will come when we'll be free
From the curse of Literacy
And when, indeed, the written word –
Like the dodo, dol'rous bird –
Will disappear. And then we'll let
All text, from book to internet,
Manuals, comics, magazines
As well as pens and fax machines
And all the wars and all the fighting
That come from us reading and writing
Wither away. Illiterately
We'll live in Peace and Harmony
And hark, instead, to tales of harvest
Read by bloody Martin Jarvis.

Part III

Short Sharp Shock

a long long way after Hilaire Belloc

Tom, who wouldn't go to school
Was found drowned in a swimming pool.

Beth was once slightly unkind
And so the Good Lord struck her blind.

Dan, who wrote on toilet walls,
Now pisses blood when Nature calls.

Alexander wet the bed.
A bolt of lightning struck him dead.

Patrick wouldn't eat his veg.
His teachers pushed him off a ledge.

Jade was horrid to her cat.
A big steam roller squashed her flat.

Ken ran screaming round the room.
Ivy now obscures his tomb.

Phyllis was quite impolite.
Her maiden aunts set her alight.

Clive once walked across the grass.
A tapeworm now lives up his arse.

Sophie made a dreadful smell.
We found her hanging in her cell.

Rufus wouldn't comb his hair.
He fried in the electric chair.

Beatrice wouldn't use her fork.
When she burned she smelled like pork.

Dorothy once kissed a boy
So is the type the gods destroy.

Audrey wouldn't blow her nose.
Policemen set fire to her clothes.

Emma's only word was 'Can't!'
She was murdered by her aunt.

Siobhan fidgeted in Church
So is no stranger to the birch.

Steve often stayed out after dark.
His death involved a great white shark.

Montmorency picked his teeth.
His life thereafter was quite brief.

When Melinda answered back
She dropped dead of a heart attack.

Mikey surfed the Internet.
A biker stabbed him for a bet.

Lucian wore a baseball cap.
Got interfered with by a chap.

When she laughed Myfanwy hissed.
Honestly, she won't be missed.

Pete, a poet, penned a stanza
And obviously he then got cancer.

Josephine wore gloves indoors.
Lions have such vicious claws.

Kate gave money to a tramp.
Her death was slow and very damp.

Sven made furniture from kits.
Choked on his tongue once prone to fits.

Molly lied about her age.
Her uncle slew her in a rage.

Leroy did a tiny fart.
His grandma stabbed him through the heart.

Bethan wouldn't clean her gun.
Her bones are now bleached by the sun.

Debs just couldn't give a fuck
So she got knocked down by a truck.

Geoffrey took 'e' at a rave.
Now occupies a shallow grave.

Honore had sex unwed.
Goodness how those knife wounds bled!

Brian was an all-round pain.
We put electrodes in his brain.

Lavinia once told a lie
And so we built her gallows high.

Manners were what Joe forgot.
We strangled him with a garotte.

Brenda simply wouldn't wash.
We beat her brains out with a cosh.

Timothy rattled his chains.
We think the dogs ate his remains.

Clare did not believe in God.
We drove nails through the little sod.

Len mocked God under his breath.
We stoned the little cunt to death.

Ermintrude presumed to breathe.
None of us bothered to grieve.

And little Kate would not obey.
But we killed her anyway.

Children come in many sizes,
While Death turns up in different guises.

Their little lives are now all spent.
Their punishments were heaven sent.

Each one of them some rule defiled.
SPARE THE ROD AND SPOIL THE CHILD.

PART IV
In Brief

Clerihew

When Paul Dacre
Goes to meet his Maker
Lord Satan in Hell
Will complain about the smell.

Love Poem

for AVC

She walks with moonlight in her hair
And growls just like a grizzly bear,
Foully invoking God Above
Along the Ley Lines of our Love.